I Want That Hat!

written by Anne Giulieri
illustrated by Beatriz Castro

T0372080

"I like that black hat," said Bob.
"It looks good!"

2

3

"Mum!" said Bob.
"I **want** that black hat!"

"That is **not** the hat
for you," said Mum.

"I like that red top,"
said Bob.
"Mum!
I **want** that red top too!"

"That is **not** the top
for you," said Mum.

"Oh no," cried Bob.
"I **want** that black hat.
I **want** that red top too!"

"No, Bob," said Mum.
"This green hat is for you.
This green top
is for you too!"

"Look!" said Mum.
"Come and see."

11

Bob looked down
into the garden.

"**Oh**!" said Bob.
"I like the green hat.
I like the green top too!"

"Look at me!" shouted Bob.
"I can play in the snow.
I can jump in the snow too!"

"This green hat
is for me," said Bob.
"This green top
is for me too!"